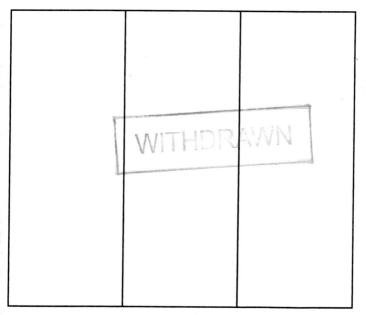

WAYLAND

First published in Great Britain in 2015 by Wayland

Copyright © Wayland 2015

Dewey Number: 822.3'3-dc23
ISBN: 978 0 7502 9211 5
Library ebook ISBN: 978 0 7502 8169 0

10 9 8 7 6 5 4 3 2 1

MIX
Paper from
responsible sources
FSC® C104740
www.fsc.org

Editor: Debbie Foy
Design: Rocket Design (East Anglia) Ltd
Illustration: Alex Paterson

Wayland
An imprint of
Hachette Children's Group
Part of Hodder & Stoughton
Carmelite House
50 Victoria Embankment
London EC4Y 0DZ

Printed and bound by CPI Group (UK) Ltd, Croydon, CR0 4YY

An Hachette UK company
www.hachette.co.uk
www.hachettechildrens.co.uk
All illustrations by Shutterstock, except 7, 13 18, 21, 26, 35, 47, 51, 59, 65, 66, 77, 89, 91.

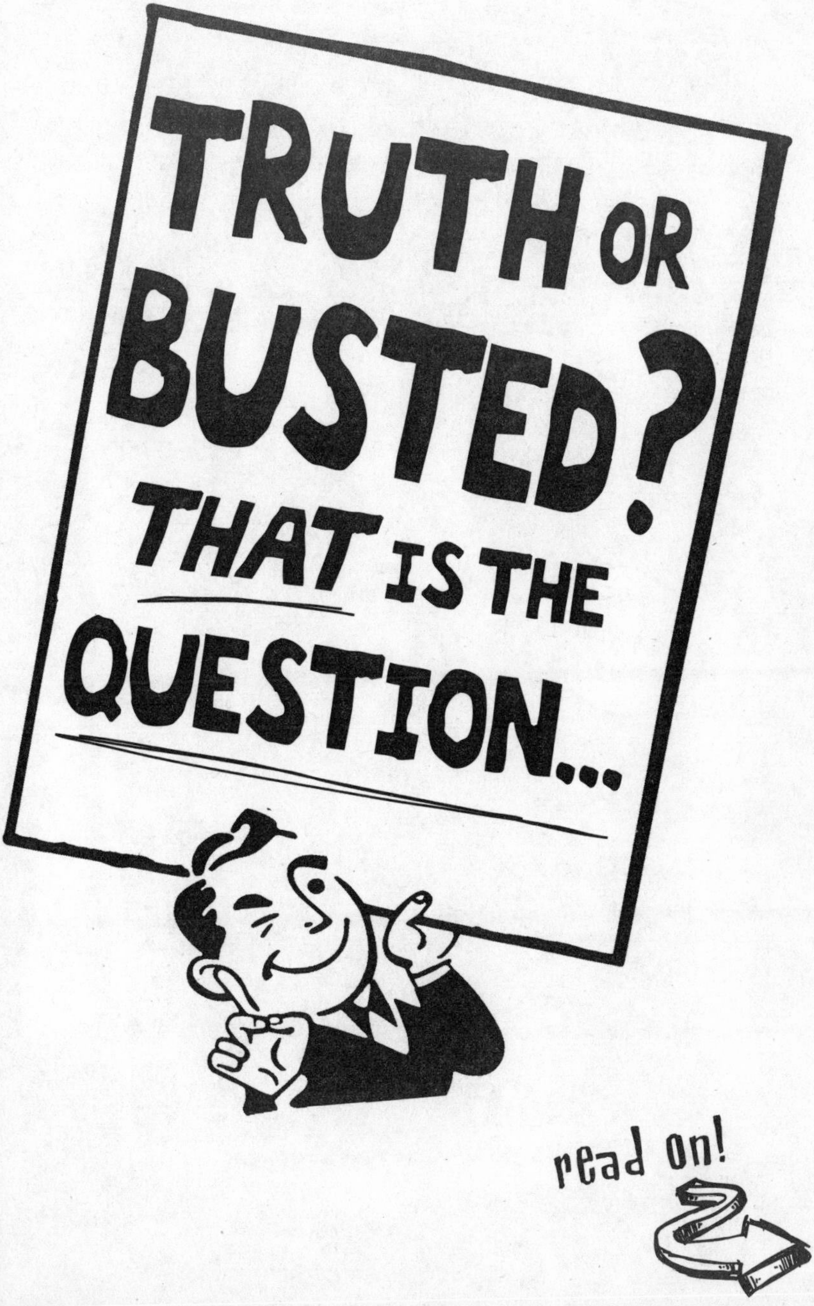

Read this bit first...!

For someone who wrote so many plays about the lives of others, there are very few actual records about Shakespeare's own life. There are really only a handful of facts we know about the world's greatest playwright...

I am a man of mystery, me.

The facts that we know are as follows:

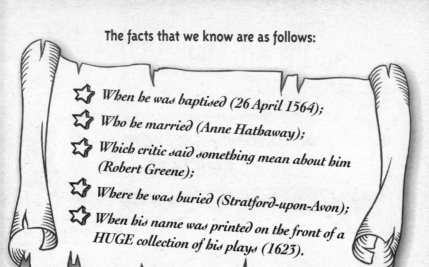

⭐ When he was baptised (26 April 1564);

⭐ Who he married (Anne Hathaway);

⭐ Which critic said something mean about him (Robert Greene);

⭐ Where he was buried (Stratford-upon-Avon);

⭐ When his name was printed on the front of a HUGE collection of his plays (1623).

All this information might be totally invaluable, but it's not exactly riveting stuff. Where are the shipwrecks and the tales of mistaken identity? Where are the battles and the romantic scenes on balconies? Where are the kings and queens and dukes and fairies? Why doesn't Shakespeare's life story have a cast of hundreds, with wonderful names like Oberon and Macbeth and Orsino and Miranda and Ariel and Romeo and Juliet and, um, Bottom?

Sadly, it doesn't. No one bothered to write it down. Not even William Shakespeare. But his fabulous plays more than make up for the lack of detail: plays fuelled by such a vivid imagination that they are still hugely popular four centuries later.

So how is anyone supposed to find out more about Shakespeare? Luckily, despite the fact that there are so few actual facts about Shakespeare, there are PLENTY of stories about him.

Are these stories TRUTH or BUSTED? THAT is the question.

read on!

So you might hear myths like...

Shakespeare was born on 23 April 1564

Everyone knows that Shakespeare's birthday is 23 April 1564. It's in all the history books and it's all over the internet.

So surely it must be true — right?

 And the truth is...

Sorry Shakespeare fans, it's just a guess. No one actually knows when William Shakespeare was born.

What we *do* know is that Wills was definitely baptised on 26 April 1564. And back in the 16th century, babies were usually baptised about three days after they were born, so 23 April is a pretty good guess.

> ## Bonus fact!
>
> *Psst! Some think that Shakespeare's fans might have just decided that it would be lovely if England's most famous playwright's birthday fell on St George's Day. (He was the patron saint of England.) So perhaps they tweaked it a bit. Who knows?*

Verdict: Possibly **TRUTH** possibly not.

(But 23 April is as good a day as any if you'd like to wish William Shakespeare a happy birthday!)

THE BARD'S <u>BEST</u> BITS
(But what did Shakespeare mean?)

THE PLAY: MACBETH

First witch: Double, double, toil and trouble, fire burn and cauldron bubble. (Act IV: Scene I)

Er... double, double, toil and trouble, fire burn and cauldron bubble. The three witches are casting a spell. Spells NEVER make sense.

Macbeth: Is this a dagger which I see before me,

The handle toward my hand? (Act II: Scene I)

Is this a dagger I can see in front of me, its handle pointing towards my hand? (It isn't, by the way. Macbeth has lost the plot just a tiny bit and is imagining it...)

DIDST THOU KNOW?

Mary Arden (1537–1608) was the daughter of a rich landowner. But she is much more famous for being William Shakepeare's mum. You might think that Arden Shakespeare – a very famous and prestigious series of books containing Shakespeare's works – was named after her.

But you'd be wrong.

It's actually named after the Forest of Arden in Warwickshire, which is the setting for one of Shakespeare's comedies – **As You Like It**.

> ## Shakespeare had SEVEN brothers and sisters

It is said that William Shakespeare came from a large family and had a whopping seven brothers and sisters. But is it true?

 And the truth is...

He really *did*. Meet the Shakespeare siblings!

Joan

was born in 1558, but sadly she died just two months later of the Black Death.

Margaret

arrived in 1562 and yet again tragedy struck a year later, when she too died. Again, the Black Death was to blame.

William

was born in 1564. To find out more about the Shakespeares' eldest son, please refer to the rest of the pages in this book!

Gilbert

was born in 1566 and then he surprised everyone by catching and *surviving* the Black Death. Hurray!

Joan

was born in 1569. (This is not a typo. The Shakespeares *did* have two daughters called Joan. Many years ago, children were often named after older brothers or sisters who had died.) She was very close to her brother William and lived to the grand old age of 77.

Anne

was born in 1571, but died in 1579 from the old enemy, the Black Death.

Richard

is a bit of a mystery. Apart from the facts that he was born in 1574 and died in 1613, little more is known about him.

Edmund

born in 1580, became… an ACTOR. But he died at the age of just 27 in London, probably from (you guessed it) the Black Death.

Verdict:

Shakespeare's dad was a butcher, a baker and a candlestick maker

Wouldn't that be totally awesome if it were true? It's poetry worthy of Shakespeare himself.

★ And the truth is...

Actually, no. He was none of these. Which is a shame, because they rhyme. However, John Shakespeare (1532–1601) *did* change his job nearly as often as he changed his pants, and here are a few of the things he *did* do for a living.

⚜ He was a glove-maker. (Handy!)

⚜ He sold wool, leather goods, malt and corn. (But not cars because they hadn't invented them.)

⚜ He drank beer. (Or rather, it was his job to taste beer and whisky to make sure it was good quality.)

⚜ He loaned money to people. (He was much richer after marrying someone whose father had POTS of money.)

⚜ He was the chief magistrate of the local town council. (This was like being the mayor. How GRAND.)

⚜ And then everything went horribly wrong and he got into debt. (Oh dear.)

Verdict: **BUSTED** but there's a little bit of truth in it.

He was a child bridegroom

Juliet (of *Romeo and Juliet* fame) was a child bride, of course. She was only 13 years old. So, was Shakespeare himself this young when he tied the knot? How shocking!

★ And the truth is...

Shakespeare was 18 when he got married, so he wasn't exactly a child, but the age of consent to marry at the time was 21. However, his bride was positively ancient by comparison — she was 26. She was also already expecting their first child*. Rather than risk upsetting everyone — it was way back in 1582, when this would have been a HUGE scandal — they got married super quick.

Verdict:  sort of.

*Susanna was born six months after the wedding. She probably didn't go to school (though she could sign her own name), married a doctor when she was 24 and had Shakespeare's first granddaughter the following year.

Shakespeare married a Hollywood film star

ANNE HATHAWAY

Pop the words 'Anne Hathaway' into a search engine and most of the results it pings back at you will be about an American actress who has appeared on stage, on TV and in a stack of films including *The Princess Diaries, Ella Enchanted* and *Les Misérables*. And she's won an Oscar, which is REALLY cool.

Fancy that. Shakespeare's wife was Proper Famous.

 And the truth is...

But Anne Hathaway the film star, who was born in 1982, is clearly not the same Anne Hathaway who married Shakespeare exactly four centuries earlier, in 1582. Because if she were, she'd be ever so wrinkly.

Verdict: **BUSTED**

unless magic face cream really has been invented.
(Oh, and the secret of everlasting life.)

DIDST THOU KNOW?

No one actually knows that much about the Anne Hathaway who became Mrs Shakespeare. But that hasn't stopped them doing a LOT of guessing.

William was **forced** to marry Anne by her family.

(No evidence.)

William **loathed** Anne.

(No evidence, although she did live in Stratford, while he spent most of his time in London, so they didn't spend much time together.)

William **immortalised** Anne in a sonnet.

(Well, he might have. And he might not. No one is sure.)

THE BARD'S BEST BITS

(But what did Shakespeare mean?)

THE PLAY: TWELFTH NIGHT

Malvolio: Be not afraid of greatness. Some are born great, some achieve greatness and some have greatness thrust upon them. (Act II: Scene V)

This means exactly what it says. Just don't be afraid of being great, OK?

Orsino: If music be the food of love, play on. (Act I: Scene I)

Let's say that love is a living thing that needs food to survive. Got that? Good. And how about if music is a type of food? In which case, a lovely melody would be just what love needs to grow. So don't put that violin/flute/electric guitar/harp/trombone/triangle down... Keep playing! Swoon...

18

WHAT? Shock. Horror. GASP!

Er, ok, keep calm everyone. As it hasn't been proven yet that aliens have abducted anyone (that we know of...), Shakespeare probably didn't take a trip in a UFO in the late 16th century. BUT, it's true that there's no trace of him or his whereabouts between 1585 (which is when his twins were baptised in Stratford) and 1592 (when London critic Robert Greene called him an 'upstart crow'). So that's SEVEN WHOLE YEARS when historical records don't make a single mention of the great man.

Nothing. Nada. Nowt.

So, if he wasn't being abducted by aliens, what did William Shakespeare *do* for seven years?

★ And the truth is...

There have been PLENTY of guesses — teacher, lawyer, traveller, actor and poacher — but the most likely answer appears to be that he spent the missing years learning how to be a playwright. He may have been collecting ideas for plots or he may have been working alongside other playwrights. And by 1592, not only had he relocated to London, a number of his plays were already being performed on stage.

Verdict:

But bizarre, huh?

Shakespeare was a ghost

By 1592, Shakespeare had moved from Stratford to London, where he was working as a playwright and an actor. In 1594, a theatre company called The Lord Chamberlain's Men (later called The King's Men) was formed and it's very likely that Shakespeare was one of the first to join.

James Burbage was in charge of the Lord Chamberlain's Men and played all the BIG roles, like Hamlet and Othello. William Kempe was the resident comic. There were a handful of other fellows, including Henry Condell and John Heminges (find out more about THEM on page 44–5).

Ahem. This is all totally fascinating, BUT WAS SHAKESPEARE A GHOST OR NOT?

⭐ And the truth is...

Mr William Shakespeare was one of the Lord Chamberlain's Men too. He wrote the plays and acted in them. But he didn't play the lead — it's rumoured that he went for the smaller roles instead, such as Adam in *As You Like It*, King Duncan in *Macbeth* and ... drumroll ... the ghost of Hamlet's father in *Hamlet*.

So, yes, Shakespeare was a ghost.

Wooooooooooo. SCARY.

Verdict: _____ **TRUTH** sort of.

21

SHAKESPEARE WROTE 38 PLAYS?

It's a pretty easy thing to work out, surely. All you have to do is count them.

Except … Shakespeare wasn't terribly good at keeping copies of his plays. And the exact number of plays that he wrote has never really been pinned down.

In the *First Folio*, the first printed collection of Shakespeare's works (see page 45), there were **36** plays.

But the *Second Folio* (a revised edition of the First Folio) included an extra two plays — *Pericles, Prince of Tyre* and *The Two Noble Kinsmen*. So that's **38** plays.

Then there's *Cardenio* (see page 72-3), which makes **39**.

Love's Labour's Won (a possible sequel to *Love's Labour's Lost*) may have been published too, making **40**.

And what about *Edward III*, which was printed anonymously in 1596? Shakespeare could have helped to write that play too, nudging the number up to **41**.

There are even rumours that Shakespeare had something to do with another 12 plays, which would make the grand total **53**. Or not.

Shakespeare: The Plays

histories

Crazy about kings? Bonkers about battles?
Fancy brushing up on your mediaeval history?
(Or Shakespeare's version, anyway.)
Then go to see a Shakespearean history!

Henry VI, Part 2

Richard III

Henry VI, Part 3

Henry VI, Part 1

King John

Richard II

Henry IV, Part 1

Henry IV, Part 2

Henry V

Henry VIII

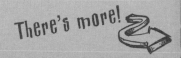

There's more!

Tragedies

Maybe you prefer strong characters that career headlong towards DOOM? Or you just love a really good weepy? Then pack a box of tissues and head for one of Shakespeare's tragedies. They weren't called that for nothing, you know. (Sob.)

Titus Andronicus

Romeo and Juliet

Julius Caesar

Hamlet

Othello

King Lear

Macbeth

Antony and Cleopatra

Timon of Athens

Coriolanus

Two Noble Kinsmen

Comedies

If you're up for a light-hearted play with plenty of comedy, loads of laughs, a sprinkling of love, with deception and mistaken identity to spice things up, then a Shakespearean comedy is the one for you!

The Taming of the Shrew

The Two Gentlemen of Verona

The Comedy of Errors

Love's Labour's Lost

A Midsummer Night's Dream

The Merchant of Venice

Much Ado About Nothing

As You Like It

The Merry Wives of Windsor

Twelfth Night

Troilus and Cressida

All's Well That Ends Well

Measure for Measure

Pericles, Prince of Tyre

Cymbeline

The Winter's Tale

The Tempest

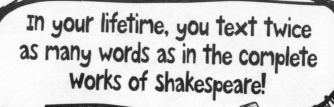

In your lifetime, you text twice as many words as in the complete works of Shakespeare!

The Complete Works of Shakespeare

Wow. That's a LOT of texting.

⭐ And the truth is...

Recent research suggests that the average mobile phone user texts about 2 million words in their lifetime. Researchers figured out that young people send around four messages per day, each of about 20 words in length. This tots up to 30,000 words per year. The report suggested that if you texted from your mid-teens to the age of 80, you would have sent a total of 1,993,200 words, which is roughly twice as many words as in *The Complete Works of Shakespeare*!

'2B or not 2B? Tht is the Q...'

But probably not as poetic.

Verdict: Probably **TRUTH** (Now put that phone down and pick up a Shakespeare play instead!)

Shakespeare named one of his most famous characters after his son

It makes total sense. Will's son was called Hamnet and he wrote about a character in one of his plays called Hamlet. Maybe he just spelt it wrong?

Am I Hamnet or Hamlet?

Search me!

⭐ And the truth is...

Shakespeare's son's name WAS sometimes spelt 'Hamlet', which was perhaps a nickname. So Shakespeare may well have named Hamlet, Prince of Denmark after his own boy. Or he may not.

Whatever, neither Hamnet nor the Prince of Denmark had happy endings. Poor Hamnet died in 1596 when he was just 11. And *Hamlet* the play, which was written five years later, is a tragedy, so there are no prizes for guessing what happens to quite a lot of the characters before the curtain falls...

Verdict: Possibly **TRUTH**

THE BARD'S BEST BITS

(But what did Shakespeare mean?)

THE PLAY: HAMLET

> **Hamlet:** To be, or not to be? That is the question. (Act III: Scene I)

This is the beginning of Hamlet's famous soliloquy in which he weighs up the pros and cons of life versus death.

> **Polonius:** Though this be madness, yet there is a method in 't. (Act II: Scene II)

Even though this is a bit bonkers, it does sort of make sense.

> **Polonius:** Neither a borrower nor a lender be;
> For loan oft loses both itself and friend, and
> borrowing dulls the edge of husbandry.
> (Act I: Scene III)

Don't borrow stuff and don't lend stuff; it'll end in tears.

Hamlet: Brevity is the soul of wit. (Act II, Scene II)

Great speakers don't have to bang on and on to get their point across.

Hamlet: In my mind's eye. (Act I: Scene II)

In my imagination. (But isn't 'mind's eye' a truly fabulous way of putting it? Nice one, Shakespeare.)

Gertrude: The lady doth protest too much, methinks.

I think the lady's overdoing it a bit. And I'm not sure I believe what she's saying.

Bonus fact!

A soliloquy is when an actor in a play talks to themselves, thereby sharing their top-secret thoughts with the entire audience. It doesn't really happen in true life, because people usually like to keep their top-secret thoughts, er, TOP SECRET. But this sort of solo speech is a very useful technique for a playwright to use, because it means that they can tell the audience exactly what characters are thinking. None of the other actors are around when the soliloquy is spoken. They aren't allowed to find out what the character's thoughts are. Why? Because they're TOP SECRET, of course.

DIDST THOU KNOW?

Shakespeare's son, Hamnet, was a TWIN. He and his sister Judith were born in 1585 and named after Shakespeare's baker friend and his wife (who were called, um, Hamnet and Judith too). So perhaps it's no coincidence that two of Shakespeare's plays, **Twelfth Night** and **The Comedy of Errors**, feature twins. So Shakespeare knew a lot about them.

In **TWELFTH NIGHT**, twins Sebastian and Viola are separated during a terrible storm, when they are shipwrecked in the kingdom of Illyria. Each believes the other to be dead. (Sniff.) But they're both alive. (Hurray!) Thinking that she'll never get a job because she's a woman, Viola dresses up as a man and goes to work for Duke Orsino. Then Viola falls in love with Orsino. (Awww.) Except he loves Lady Olivia, who is in mourning and not thinking about love at all ... until she meets Viola (who is dressed as a man, remember) and falls in love with her. So, Orsino loves Olivia who loves Viola who loves Orsino. Got that? And when Sebastian arrives on the scene, things become EVEN MORE complicated (and very, very funny).

THE COMEDY OF ERRORS has not one but TWO sets of twins in it. And they're identical. And what's more, they've got nearly identical names too... Meet Antipholus of Syracuse and his twin brother Antipholus of Ephesus, who were separated at birth. And meet their twin slaves, Dromio of Syracuse and Dromio of Ephesus, who were also separated at birth. When Antipholus and Dromio of Syracuse travel to Ephesus and bump into the people who know Antipholus and Dromio of Ephesus, they are mistaken for their twin brothers and everything becomes very, very silly indeed. Just as the play's title promises, it's definitely a comedy and there are plenty of errors.

The word 'sonnet' means 'little song'

Really, truly, honestly?

⭐ And the truth is...

This is absolutely and utterly correct. It comes from the Italian word 'sonetto', which should not be confused with any type of ice cream.

A Shakespearean sonnet is a poem made up of 14 lines of iambic pentameter, which is a fancy way of saying that each line is ten syllables long. But the REALLY clever bit is that all 154 Shakespearean sonnets rhyme in exactly the same way.

Sonnet 18 is one of the most famous. It's fabulously romantic, which means that it's a super-popular reading at weddings. It's about someone who is supposed to be waaaaay more beautiful than a summer's day. And while summer ends, love will go on FOR EVER. Awww.

Verdict: _____ TRUTH _____

Sonnet 18

Shall I compare thee to a summer's day?
Thou art more lovely and more temperate;
Rough winds do shake the darling buds of May,
And summer's lease hath all too short a date;

Sometime too hot the eye of heaven shines,
And often is his gold complexion dimm'd;
And every fair from fair sometime declines,
By chance or nature's changing course untrimm'd;

But thy eternal summer shall not fade,
Nor lose possession of that fair thou ow'st;
Nor shall Death brag thou wander'st in his shade,
When in eternal lines to time thou grow'st:

So long as men can breathe or eyes can see,
So long lives this, and this gives life to thee.

William Shakespeare

A Right Pair!

ROMEO and JULIET
From the play
'*Romeo and Juliet*'

What happens?

Romeo is a member of the Montague family. Juliet's a Capulet. The Montagues and the Capulets REALLY don't get on. Then Romeo and Juliet fall deeply in love... How can they be together when their two families are at war? It's a tricky one. (Clue: it doesn't end well.)

Truth or busted?

Romeo and Juliet are totally made up. (Sorry.) The Bard was inspired by a poem about Romeus and Juliet by Arthur Brooke, which was then retold by William Painter. Once the story had been given the Shakespeare treatment, it went on to become properly famous. But it's still not true.

Juliet's Wall

The story of Romeo and Juliet might be complete fiction, but Verona — where the play is set — is very real. One house is said to be the actual home of the Capulets. Its entrance wall might be full of graffiti, but they are all messages of love.

Awww. In the courtyard, lovesick visitors stick letters to the walls, hoping that their true love will one day read them. It's not a terribly good idea though. The letters are removed almost as fast as they are stuck up.

Comedy, Tragedy or History?

Plays don't get more tragic than this. Take tissues. LOTS AND LOTS OF TISSUES.

Shakespeare wrote movie screenplays

WOW. Fancy writing screenplays BEFORE cinema had even been invented!

 And the truth is...

Er, no. Of *course* he didn't write screenplays. He was a playwright, not a time-traveller. But Shakespeare did write playscripts that have been used to turn his plays into blockbuster movies.

Take *Romeo and Juliet*, for example. So far, more than FORTY different movies based on Shakespeare's playscript have been made. Two have been mega-successful:

Romeo and Juliet (1968) was directed by Franco Zeffirelli, starred Leonard Whiting and Olivia Hussey and won two Oscars.

William Shakespeare's Romeo and Juliet (1996) — just in case anyone didn't know who'd written it, obvs — was directed by Baz Luhrmann and starred Leonardo diCaprio and Claire Danes. It took $147 million at the box office worldwide.

Shakespeare would've been proud.

Verdict: Sort of **TRUTH**

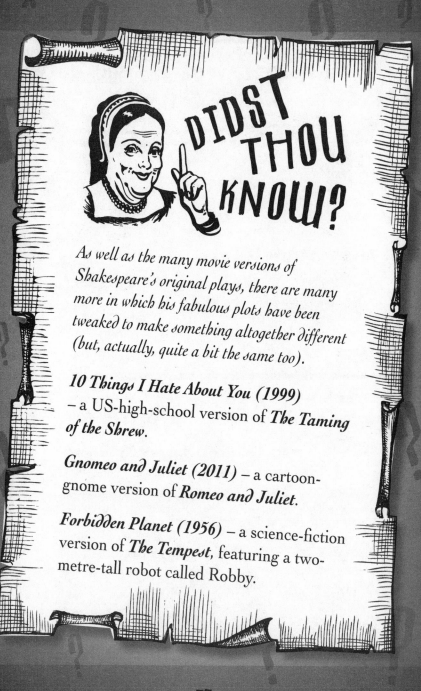

DIDST THOU KNOW?

As well as the many movie versions of Shakespeare's original plays, there are many more in which his fabulous plots have been tweaked to make something altogether different (but, actually, quite a bit the same too).

10 Things I Hate About You (1999) – a US-high-school version of ***The Taming of the Shrew***.

Gnomeo and Juliet (2011) – a cartoon-gnome version of ***Romeo and Juliet***.

Forbidden Planet (1956) – a science-fiction version of ***The Tempest***, featuring a two-metre-tall robot called Robby.

Shakespeare wrote the musical *West Side Story*

Would that be the *West Side Story* that premiered in 1957 on Broadway, 341 years after Shakespeare died?

Er, yes.

So how could Shakespeare have written it? (Unless it took a very, very long time to rehearse.)

 And the truth is...

Well, he didn't and he did.

Shakespeare didn't write the actual musical — Arthur Laurents wrote the book and Leonard Bernstein the music, with the lyrics by Stephen Sondheim and the choreography by Jerome Robbins — but there's no question that *West Side Story* WAS inspired by Shakespeare's *Romeo and Juliet*. When the names and the locations are stripped away, they're basically the same story.

Apart from the endings.*

Verdict: Sort of  TRUTH

*Not telling. Watch them both to find out.

When the author of this book saw the Royal Shakespeare Company perform Romeo and Juliet on stage, the cast were dressed in the style of West Side Story in 1950s clothes. So the play was paying homage to the musical that was based on the book that was based on the play. Cool, huh?

Romeo and Juliet v West Side Story

	Romeo & Juliet	West Side Story
Leading man	Romeo	Tony
Leading lady	Juliet	Maria
Opposite sides	Montagues and Capulets	Jets and Sharks
Location	Verona, Italy	Upper West Side, New York City, USA
When?	1597	1950s
First glimpse	A party	A gym
Street fight	Yes	Yes
View from above	Balcony	Fire escape
Wedding	Yes	No
Academy Awards	Yes, a few	Yes, a lot
Singing and dancing ...	No	Yes
Happy ever after?	No. (Take two boxes of tissues.)	No. (Take one box of tissues.)

THE BARD'S <u>BEST</u> BITS
(But what did Shakespeare mean?)

THE PLAY: ROMEO AND JULIET

Juliet: *O Romeo, Romeo! Wherefore art thou, Romeo?*
(Act II: Scene II)

Oh, Romeo, Romeo! Why are you Romeo? Why couldn't you be someone else? (Romeo and Juliet's two families do NOT get on. It wasn't a terribly good idea for them to fall in love, you know.)

Romeo: *But, soft! What light through yonder window breaks?*
It is the east, and Juliet is the sun.
(Act II: Scene II)

Hang on a minute. What's that light shining from the window over there? It's the east and Juliet is the sun. (Which, um, sort of means that Juliet shines as brightly as the rising sun, which is another way of saying that she's VERY beautiful.)

Shakespeare didn't write his own plays

GASP. What a thing to say! The man was a geeeeeenius.

⭐ And the truth is...

Many people DON'T believe that Shakespeare wrote the 38 plays that he's credited with writing. Instead, they believe that Someone Else is the greatest playwright in history. They just can't agree on who it was...

Here is a list of The Usual Suspects:

Edward de Vere (the seventeenth Earl of Oxford)

This royal fellow is a favourite among conspiracy theorists. Except he died in 1604, before Macbeth *and a bunch of other plays were written.*

Turn over for more suspects

Christopher Marlowe

Playwright and poet and supposedly a spy too – shhhh – the author of Doctor Faustus was an expert at tragedy and is said to have influenced Shakespeare. But he died in Very Mysterious Circumstances in 1593… Unless, he didn't die then at all, but instead escaped to another country and wrote a LOT of plays that, because he was 'dead', he couldn't claim as his own.

Sir Francis Bacon

Wow. He was already a scientist, a star in the royal court and a philosopher. How did he find time to be a playwright too?

Mary Sidney Herbert, Countess of Pembroke

This über-talented woman was a terrific writer AND lived at exactly the right time to have written all of Shakespeare's plays. But no one would have watched plays by a woman, so she used Shakespeare's name instead. Apparently.

Elizabeth 1

Yes, really. Some think that William Shakespeare was simply a front for Queen Elizabeth I, who was actually the one who wrote all the plays. As well as being in charge of an entire country and defeating the Spanish Armada, of course.

So... Whodunnit?

Actually, there is evidence that playwrights often did work together in Shakespearean times. This was a perfectly normal thing to happen.

John Fletcher is said to have co-written *The Two Noble Kinsmen* (his name appears on the title page), *Henry VIII* and *The History of Cardenio* (see page 72-3) with Shakespeare. He even wrote a sequel to Shakespeare's *The Taming of the Shrew* after the Bard's death. So perhaps Shakespeare did have a bit of help with some of his plays.

But most people believe that William Shakespeare wasn't a woman or a queen or a spy or a scientist or an earl. He was a chap who wrote plays and came from Stratford-upon-Avon.

Verdict: Mostly **BUSTED** but a tiny bit **TRUTH**

Shakespeare's plays were available in all good bookshops while he was alive

Oh yes they were.

⭐ And the truth is...

Oh no they weren't.

Shakespeare wanted people to watch his plays at the theatre. He didn't want them to buy a copy of the script and read it at home. And he certainly didn't want other theatre companies to use the scripts to put on Shakespeare's plays. Or that's the theory behind the fact that Shakespeare didn't publish them.

And there's another reason Shakespeare didn't publish the plays … they weren't his to publish. He belonged to a group of actors called The Lord Chamberlain's Men (and later The King's Men). *They* owned the copyright.

But Shakespeare's plays were published — seven years after he died. Fellow actors from The King's Men, John

Heminges and Henry Condell, did everyone a favour and collected the plays together, publishing *Mr. William Shakespeares Comedies, Histories, & Tragedies* in 1623. The work contained 36 plays — *Pericles*, *Prince of Tyre* and *The Two Noble Kinsmen* were missing — and is the most reliable record of Shakespeare's plays. Without it, many of the plays may never have made it into print. Yikes.

In the dedication, Heminges and Condell said that they were publishing the plays NOT for self-profit or fame, but to keep the memory of a friend and fellow actor alive.

How lovely!

NOTE:

There really was no apostrophe in Shakespeares on the original collection.

Verdict: — **BUSTED** —

THE BARD'S BEST BITS
(But what did Shakespeare mean?)

THE PLAY: A MIDSUMMER NIGHT'S DREAM

Lysander: *The course of true love never did run smooth.* (Act I: Scene I)

True love is never straightforward. There are always pesky problems to overcome before a lovely gooey happy ending with hearts and flowers and chocolates and maybe an orchestra playing something by Puccini in the distance.

Oberon: *Ill met by moonlight, proud Titania.* (Act II: Scene I)

I can think of other people I'd rather meet by moonlight, proud Titania. (Oberon and Titania are not getting on. Obvs.)

Puck: *Lord, what fools these mortals be!* (Act III: Scene II)

People are idiots. (Tell us something we don't know, Mr Shakespeare.)

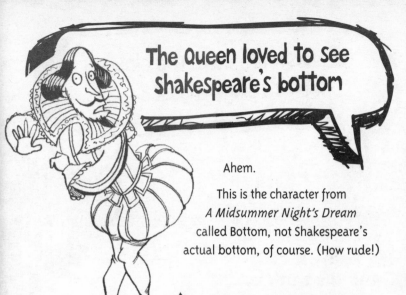

The Queen loved to see Shakespeare's bottom

Ahem.

This is the character from *A Midsummer Night's Dream* called Bottom, not Shakespeare's actual bottom, of course. (How rude!)

⭐ And the truth is...

Queen Elizabeth I was a big fan of the arts. And she loved Shakespeare's plays so much that she was a royal patron of the theatre company he belonged to — the Chamberlain's Men.

It wasn't the done thing for Elizabeth I to visit the theatre with the general public. So instead, the Lord Chamberlain's Men played at the royal court to entertain the queen and her courtiers. *Love's Labour's Lost* was performed before Queen Elizabeth in 1597. And while there are no records to show that she saw a performance of *A Midsummer Night's Dream* it was written during her lifetime, so the chances are, she did see it ... and Shakespeare's Bottom.

Verdict: **TRUTH** probably.

47

Shakespeare built The Globe theatre single-handedly

A gifted playwright AND a master builder? Wow. Shakespeare ROCKED.

★ And the truth is...

Er, no. Shakespeare had very little to do with it.

In the late 16th century, The Lord Chamberlain's Men had a problem. The lease on their theatre — called, er, The Theatre — expired and even though they found other places to act, there was nowhere the company could call home.

So they bought a plot of land beside the River Thames, which was quite near to rival theatre The Rose. Then timber by timber, they dismantled The Theatre, carried it across the river, built it on the other side and renamed it The Globe.

Shakespeare *did* contribute towards the cost of building The Globe in exchange for shares in the new theatre, but that was all. Most of the hard work was done by Cuthbert and Richard Burbage — James Burbage's sons.

Verdict: __Mostly__ **BUSTED**

Shakespeare burned down The Globe theatre

Why on earth would Shakespeare burn down the very theatre where his plays were enjoyed by thousands of people? That's MADNESS.

 And the truth is...

Erm, yes. Shakespeare was a little bit responsible for the fire that destroyed the first Globe Theatre. But only because he wrote the play that was being performed when the fire started.

It happened on 29 June 1613, when a cannon fired onstage during Shakespeare's *Henry VIII*.

BOOM.

The thatched roof caught fire.

CRACKLE.

And The Globe theatre burnt to the ground in under two hours.

OOPS!

They rebuilt The Globe soon after, but this time with a tiled roof.

Sensible.

Verdict: Sort of TRUTH but Shakespeare didn't do it on purpose.

51

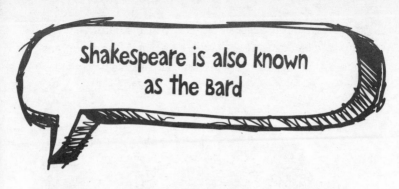

Shakespeare is also known as the Bard

What sort of a nickname is that? It rhymes with lard, yes. But what does it even *mean*?

 And the truth is...

No kidding. That really is William Shakespeare's nickname.

Many years ago, a bard was a type of minstrel-poet. Celtic bards composed and sang verses to celebrate big events (or to praise or poke fun at people). In Wales, a bard was a poet honoured at Eisteddfod — one of Europe's largest and oldest cultural festivals. But the word can also be used to mean any poet.

Shakespeare was a poet as well as a playwright. During his lifetime, he wrote 154 sonnets (see page 32), two long narrative poems and a number of other poems too. As well as the 38 — or thereabouts — plays, of course. (He was clearly a very busy man.)

But it was an event in 1769 that inspired Shakespeare's nickname. That year, a famous Shakespearean actor named David Garrick organised a Shakespeare Jubilee to be held in Stratford-upon-Avon to celebrate the 200th anniversary of his birth. (As that was in 1564, which was 205 years earlier, presumably the event took a while to organise.)

Cannon were fired, church bells were rung, a statue of

Shakespeare was unveiled at the Town Hall and Garrick himself performed his *Ode to Shakespeare* — a poem in his honour. And from then on Shakespeare fever heated up and he began to be known as the Bard of Avon or simply … the Bard.

Don't call me sweetie!

Verdict: **TRUTH**

Shakespeare was also known as the Bard of Stratford and the Swan of Avon, but perhaps the most beautiful nickname of them all was given to him by fellow playwright Ben Jonson, who called him the Sweet Swan of Avon.

Shakespeare's *Richard III* was just like the real king

Richard III is perhaps Shakespeare's most famous bad guy. He lies. He murders. He doesn't let ANYTHING get between him and the throne.

Audience: *boos loudly*

Richard III at the Battle of Bosworth

But he's not *totally* unlikeable. He's clever and witty. He delights in making fun of his victims. He's a bit of a show-off too. He's HUGE fun to watch.

Audience: *cheers wildly*

The thing is, Shakespeare never actually *met* Richard III. He didn't even live in the same century as him. In fact, Shakespeare wrote *Richard III* a whopping 106 years after the king died at the Battle of Bosworth.

Audience: *gasps in amazement*

read on!

So how did Shakespeare know ANYTHING about Richard III?

Simple. He based his Richard III on the Tudor opinion of the old king. After Richard III died at the Battle of Bosworth in 1485, Tudor King Henry VII wanted to look good, so he made sure that the old king looked VERY bad. And the idea that Richard III was a hunchbacked, power-mad despot stuck fast.

Audience: *tuts*

I'm really a nice chap – honest!

And the truth is...

Well, Richard III wasn't a hunchback, for a start. He suffered from scoliosis of the spine, which would have made one shoulder look a little higher than the other. And it's NEVER been proven that he murdered his nephews — Prince Edward and Prince Richard — in the Tower of London. Instead, he introduced laws that gave justice to the poor as well as the rich, wrote laws in English (which everyone spoke) instead of Latin (which everyone didn't) and introduced the bail system. So he might actually have been an OK sort of chap.

Except, it was Shakespeare's job to keep theatregoers transfixed and maybe he figured that a nice king was never going to be half as much fun to watch as an evil maniac. So he turned Richard III into a really fabulous bad guy instead.

Audience: *applauds wildly*

Verdict: — BUSTED —

THE PLAY: RICHARD III

Richard III: *Now is the winter of our discontent Made glorious summer by this son of York.*
(Act I: Scene I)

Now our dark and wintry unhappiness has ended, and been turned into bright and summery happiness by Edward IV (who belonged to the House of York, like Richard III).

Richard III: *A horse, a horse, my kingdom for a horse!*
(Act V: Scene IV)

I'd swap my kingdom for a horse any day of the week! (At this point, he's pretty desperate.)

Shakespeare bequeathed his wife his second-best bed

Is that ALL? What sort of a world-renowned playwright and most famous Shakespearean EVER leaves his wife just his SECOND-BEST BED and NOTHING ELSE?

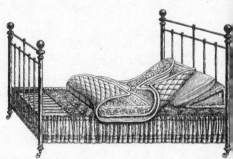

★ And the truth is...

Erm, yes. That's exactly what Shakespeare did.

BUT, the second-best bed wasn't as bad as it sounds. It was the bed William and Anne had slept in all their married lives, so it was kind of special.

Besides, according to the law at the time, Anne was already entitled to one third of Shakespeare's estate and could live in their house for the rest of her life. So she wasn't penniless.

There's no record of who was bequeathed the best bed. But as that was the bed usually kept for guests, perhaps it would have been a bit cobwebby anyway.

Verdict: **TRUTH**

There were no women in Shakespeare's plays

How silly. There are PLENTY of women in Shakespeare's plays. What about Cleopatra, Cordelia, Cressida, Desdemona, Goneril, Hermia, Hero, Hermione, Imogen, Isabella, Juliet, Katherina, Lady Macbeth, Olivia, Ophelia, Portia, Rosalind, the Three Witches, Titania and Viola, to name just a few?

 ## And the truth is...

Even though there were plenty of roles for women in Shakespeare's plays, when they were first performed, all of the parts — and here's the shocker — were played by MEN.

In Shakespearean times, people thought that acting wasn't something that a lady should do. And the Puritans, who were in charge afterwards, didn't like ANYONE to perform in theatres. It wasn't until 1660, when Charles II became king, that women were allowed to act alongside men.

And quite right too.

Verdict:

THE PLAY: AS YOU LIKE IT

Jaques: All the world's a stage,
And all the men and women merely players.
They have their exits and their entrances,
And one man in his time plays many parts...
(Act II: Scene VII)

The whole world is a stage and all men and women simply actors. They each have their times to leave and times to appear and one man in his lifetime will play many different roles. (So there you go. Shakespeare says that life's a play and you're actually onstage, right now. Take a bow!)

Touchstone: The fool doth think he is wise, but the wise man knows himself to be a fool
(Act V: Scene I)

Only a fool thinks he's clever. It takes a wise man to know that he's a fool. (Sensible words from Mr Shakespeare there.)

One of Shakespeare's relatives was hanged for treason

Yeah, right.

 And the truth is...

William Arden was Will Shakespeare's mother's second cousin, which means that William Shakespeare was William Arden's second cousin once removed. Got that? Good. Because William Arden's son was called Edward Arden. So he was Shakespeare's, um ... very distant relative.

And THEN there was John Somerville. He was Edward Arden's son-in-law, who was not Shakespeare's blood relative at all, but a whole heap of trouble. Somerville is said to have cooked up a plot to assassinate Queen Elizabeth I.

But after telling people about his plan, Somerville was arrested and tortured, before confessing to the plot — and blaming his father-in-law too. Then, Somerville was sentenced to death for treason.

It was curtains for poor old Edward Arden too. He was hanged, drawn and quartered, even though he may have been completely innocent. Yikes.

Verdict: Sadly **TRUTH**

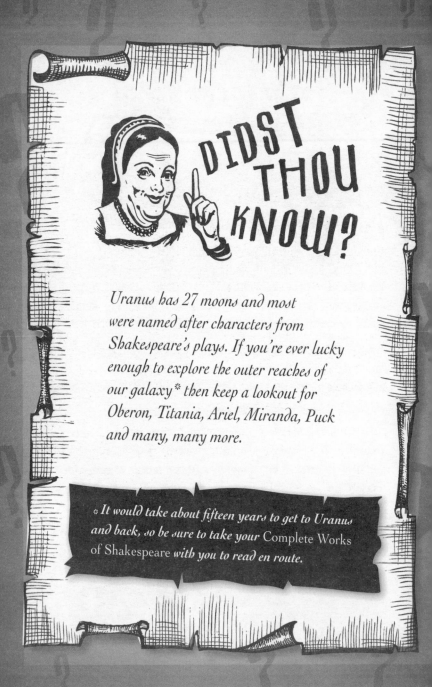

DIDST THOU KNOW?

Uranus has 27 moons and most were named after characters from Shakespeare's plays. If you're ever lucky enough to explore the outer reaches of our galaxy* then keep a lookout for Oberon, Titania, Ariel, Miranda, Puck and many, many more.

* It would take about fifteen years to get to Uranus and back, so be sure to take your Complete Works of Shakespeare with you to read en route.

Twelfth Night was first performed on Twelfth Night

Twelfth Night is the twelfth night after Christmas, also known as Epiphany. It's traditionally the day that the Christmas tree and the tinsel are taken down and it signals the end of the Christmas celebrations.

Many think Shakespeare may have written the play as a finale to the Christmas season. So was *Twelfth Night* first performed then?

And the truth is...
No.

Twelfth Night was first performed on 2 February 1602. And that's the thirty-ninth night. But this Shakespearean comedy would brighten up any day of the year, so presumably no one minded.

Verdict:  BUSTED

A Right Pair!

MACBETH and LADY MACBETH

From the play
Macbeth

What happens?

When Macbeth meets a trio of witches, he believes their prophecy that he will become King of Scotland. Except he ends up doing rather a lot of bad things to make the prophecy come true — egged on by his wife, Lady Macbeth.

Truth or busted?

Macbeth, King of Scotland really did exist. He lived in the eleventh century. But that's where the similarities between Shakespeare's Macbeth and the real king end. While the Macbeth in the play is a power-crazed, murderous maniac, the REAL Macbeth was a kind, generous king. He reigned for 17 years, while in the play, it's hardly any time at all.

Lady Macbeth existed too. In real life she was a queen, but there's no evidence to show that she was as wicked or as mad as her character, or that she spent all her time trying to get her husband to commit regicide*.

Don't say the M word!

Many actors and theatre folk prefer to call this THE SCOTTISH PLAY, because the name MACBETH is said to be a tiny bit unlucky. (Unless it's said during the play itself, of course. Presumably because it would be a bit difficult to act an entire play without mentioning the lead character's name.) There are lots of theories behind this odd superstition, such as suggesting the play is unlucky because the witches' incantations are REAL SPELLS. (Ooooh.)

Comedy, Tragedy or History?

Tragedy, most definitely. (And a whole lot of ambition, greed, blood and DEATH besides.)

Do you think I should?

Go on then!

> * Regicide does not mean killing someone called Reg. It means the killing of a king.

Shakespeare could NOT spell his own surname

He wrote a million beautiful words. Of course he could spell his own surname. Or could he...?

⭐ And the truth is...

Shakespeare COULD spell his own surname. He just couldn't stick to the same spelling. Here are just a few of the different ways he wrote it.

Shackper
Shakespeyre
Shakysper
Shappere
Shaxkspere
Shaxpeer
Shexpere
Shaxberd...

Ooops!

There are at least another 70 versions.

Bizarrely, the one spelling that no one is entirely sure that he used is — you guessed it — 'Shakespeare'.

Verdict:

TRUTH

Shakespeare was an Elizabethan playwright

Of course he was. Everyone knows that Elizabeth I watched Shakespeare's plays.

⭐ And the truth is...

It's true that Shakespeare is most often linked with Elizabeth I (1533–1603), but he was also popular during the reign of James I (1603–1625), which makes him a Jacobean playwright too.

I'm an Elizabethan, you know.

Even though a lot of Shakespeare's plays were first performed during the reign of Elizabeth I, a lot weren't. *The Tempest, Macbeth, King Lear* and *Othello* are just four of the plays that premiered when James I was on the throne.

Really? I thought you were Jacobean...

So, strictly speaking, Shakespeare was both an Elizabethan AND a Jacobean playwright.

Verdict: TRUTH but also BUSTED

67

A BRIEF HISTORY OF SHAKESPEARE'S GLOBE THEATRE

The first Globe theatre was BUILT in London on the Southbank of the Thames over Christmas 1598 and was already hosting performances by the beginning of the following year.

Wow!

Then in 1613 the thatched roof caught fire during a performance and it BURNT down. And it was all Shakespeare's fault…
(Or was it? See page 50.)

Oh Dear!

But it was REBUILT soon after (with a tiled roof this time).

Hurray!

Then the Puritans closed The Globe down in 1642.

Spoilsports!

The poor, abandoned Globe was DEMOLISHED in 1644.

Boo!

And then there was no Globe theatre at all for hundreds of years, until American actor, director and producer and all-round Shakespearean champion Sam Wanamaker decided that it would be a brilliant idea to rebuild The Globe yet again, EXACTLY as it was in Shakespeare's day (apart from fire exits and other safety features that didn't exist back then). He persuaded lots of other Shakespeare fans that this was a brilliant idea and in 1997, Shakespeare's Globe was officially opened by Queen Elizabeth II.

Three Cheers!

Shakespeare's Globe Theatre is still open to anyone who'd like to experience just what it was like to visit the Globe Theatre four centuries ago or anyone who'd just like to see a REALLY good play.

Encore!

The rebuilt Shakespeare's Globe theatre, opened in 1997

Shakespeare's Globe theatre stands in the same spot as the original

The Shakespeare Globe Trust spent years researching the original Globe, so they could make as faithful a reconstruction of the original as possible. This was NOT easy. Details of the original theatre were VERY sketchy. But with some guesswork, they came up with architect's plans for the new theatre that everyone was happy with. All they had to do now to be totally authentic was to build it in the same place.

★ And the truth is...

The Shakespeare Globe Trust couldn't build the new theatre in the same place as the original for the simple reason that THERE WAS ALREADY ANOTHER BUILDING THERE. And they could hardly knock that down. So the new Globe was built a few hundred metres away.

Verdict: **BUSTED** (but it's pretty close.)

THE BARD'S <u>BEST</u> BITS
(But what did Shakespeare mean?)

THE PLAY: ANTONY AND CLEOPATRA

Cleopatra: My salad days, when I was green in judgement. (Scene I: Act V)

When I was young and inexperienced. (So absolutely nothing to do with lettuce then.)

Enobarbus: Age cannot wither her, nor custom stale

Her infinite variety

(Act II: Scene II)

She might get older but she won't be any less fabulous, and there are so many different sides to her personality that she'll never be boring. Awww.

Shakespeare LOST one of his plays

How terribly careless of him. Fancy losing an entire play!

How did he do that...? Did he accidentally leave the playscript on a train? (Er, no. Trains hadn't been invented.) Did he forget to back up his computer and lose the file in a catastrophic hard-disk failure? (Nope. Computers hadn't been invented either.) Maybe he accidentally threw it out with the rubbish? (Possibly. Elizabethan scavengers were supposed to be pretty good at removing rubbish of any value.)

And the truth is...

No one knows.

But it is a true fact that The King's Men (see page 20) performed a play called *The History of Cardenio* in 1613. It was based on a story in *Don Quixote* by Cervantes. And apparently — *drumroll* — the play was written by Shakespeare and fellow playwright John Fletcher.

Are you keeping up?

Excellent.

No copies of *The History of Cardenio* have ever been found, but a play called *Double Falsehood* was performed over a hundred years later in 1727. It was written by Lewis Theobald, but is said to have been based on the lost play.

Then, in the 21st century, something truly FABULOUS happened. Modern playwrights, Gregory Doran and Antonio Alama took Theobald's play and, mixing it up a bit with the original *Don Quixote* story, recreated Shakespeare and Fletcher's play.

They called it simply *Cardenio* and in 2011 it became the first (almost) brand-new Shakespearean play to premiere in four hundred years.

Verdict: but they sort of found it again.

Shakespeare died on his birthday

Awwww. What a TERRIBLE way to celebrate your 52nd birthday.

Another slice of cake William?

No thanks, I feel a little headache coming on.

★ And the truth is...

No one is actually sure if 23 April was William Shakespeare's birthday or not (see page 6).

It's said that he was out partying with Ben Jonson the playwright, poet and critic and another poet called Michael Drayton when he caught a fever and swiftly died, so perhaps they were celebrating Shakespeare's birthday. Perhaps not.

Whatever the case, it is a true fact that William Shakespeare died on 23 April 1616.

Verdict: Possibly 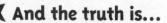 TRUTH

THE BARD'S BEST BITS

(But what did Shakespeare mean?)

THE PLAY: JULIUS CAESAR

Soothsayer: Beware the Ides of March.
(Act I: Scene II)

Beware 15 March. (The Romans did not have numbered days of the month. Instead they measured time depending on the moon's phases. The Ides were when the full moon appeared.) But whatever the day is called, the fortune-teller is warning Caesar to be very careful then... Why? Watch (or read) the play and find out!

Antony: Friends, Romans, countrymen, lend me your ears. I come to bury Caesar, not to praise him. (Act III: Scene II)

Listen, everyone. I'm here to bury Caesar. I'm not going to tell you how fabulous he was. (He's promised Brutus that he won't do this and turn the crowd against Brutus. But he does praise him anyway, with very skilful word play. Clever old Mark Antony.)

Shakespeare never had his portrait painted

Four centuries ago, there was no fancy technology for recording people's images — paintings, engravings and sculptures were all that was available. And because these weren't cheap to produce, only the rich could afford them.

There's no record of Shakespeare ever commissioning his own portrait. And neither did anyone bother making a note of what he looked like. Tsk. It was only after his death, when he became super-famous, that portraits cropped up everywhere. The problem was — which were authentic and which were fakes?

⭐ And the truth is...

Experts say that only the engraving by Martin Droeshout that appears on the First Folio (see page 22) and the monument in Holy Trinity Church in Stratford are DEFINITELY of Shakespeare. But there are many, many more images and sculptures that no one is quite sure about... Some portraits were supposedly painted of the playwright in true life — if so, they may actually show what the Bard looked like. But there are many more portraits that were painted after his death — these were either copied from earlier pictures or painted from memory, making them less reliable.

So if you want to know what Shakespeare really looked like, check out Droeshout's engraving or the half-statue in Stratford.

And then take everything else with a pinch of salt.

Verdict:

Shakespeare had his ear pierced

Earrings were quite fashionable in the late 1500s and poets especially were said to wear them. So if he had an earring, then Shakespeare wouldn't have been the only one with a pierced ear.

And the truth is...

Shakespeare IS wearing an earring in his left ear in a portrait (probably) painted by John Taylor in the 1600s. (It's a lovely gold hoop, don't you know.) Except, the portrait is only PROBABLY of Shakespeare and not DEFINITELY of Shakespeare, so we don't actually know if he DID wear an earring.

Or not.

But he might have.

We're just not sure.

Probably | possibly

Verdict: TRUTH _____ BUSTED

 **Bonus fact!** *Sailors used to wear a single gold earring. This wasn't just to look good. It was so that, if they died at sea, the earring could be sold to pay for a funeral.*

78

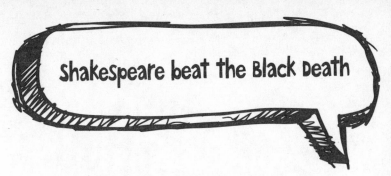

Shakespeare beat the Black Death

The Black Death was rife in Shakespeare's day. It was a particularly deadly sort of plague and outbreaks happened horribly often. The death rate was high and death from the Black Death was QUICK and NASTY. (Let's not go into details, in case you've just eaten.)

So how did Shakespeare fare in these disease-ridden times?

 ## And the truth is...

Shakespeare did amazingly well to avoid the Black Death.

One of the worst outbreaks happened in 1603, when the disease killed nearly 40,000 Londoners, and then it returned in 1608. Both times, the Globe theatre was closed to prevent the spread of disease.

But this wasn't the closest that Shakespeare came to the Black Death. Three of his sisters, a brother and his own son died from the disease when it swept through Stratford.

But not Shakespeare.

Verdict:

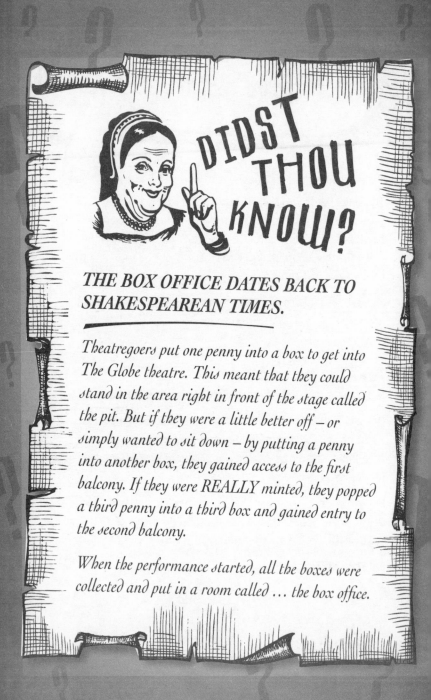

DIDST THOU KNOW?

THE BOX OFFICE DATES BACK TO SHAKESPEAREAN TIMES.

Theatregoers put one penny into a box to get into The Globe theatre. This meant that they could stand in the area right in front of the stage called the pit. But if they were a little better off – or simply wanted to sit down – by putting a penny into another box, they gained access to the first balcony. If they were REALLY minted, they popped a third penny into a third box and gained entry to the second balcony.

When the performance started, all the boxes were collected and put in a room called ... the box office.

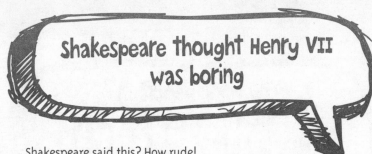

Shakespeare thought Henry VII was boring

Shakespeare said this? How rude!

★ And the truth is...

There's no evidence that Shakespeare ever said anything of the kind. (Insulting a monarch was a very silly thing to do anyway. Unless you actually WANTED to be hanged, drawn and quartered, that is.) But if you take a look at the list of King Henrys that ruled England between 1399 and 1547 who William Shakespeare DID write plays about, there is A Certain Someone The Seventh missing...

Henry IV, Part 1
Henry IV, Part 2
Henry V
Henry VI, Part 1
Henry VI, Part 2
Henry VI, Part 3
Henry VIII

Hmmmm!

So maybe there's a tiny bit of truth in it. Or maybe — as Shakespeare wrote his *Henry VI* plays before he wrote *Henry V* — he just hadn't got round to poor old *Henry VII* before he died.

Verdict: Only the Bard knew the answer.

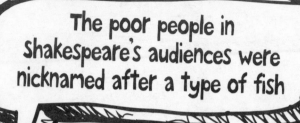

The poor people in Shakespeare's audiences were nicknamed after a type of fish

Ha ha!

Hilarious.

★ And the truth is...

It's true. The poorer members of the audience couldn't afford to pay for a seat at The Globe theatre. Instead, they paid just one penny each to stand in the pit, which was the area just below the stage. (It cost more to sit down on one of the balconies around the theatre — see page 80.) There, they gawped up at the actors and became known as groundlings, which, in the 16th and 17th centuries, was the word for a small fish with a big mouth. It might also have been partly because these audience members stood on the ground.

By the beginning of the 17th century, the term groundlings was so well known that Will Shakespeare even gave them a shout-out in *Hamlet*.

> HAMLET: *Oh, it offends me to the soul to hear a robustious periwig-pated fellow tear a passion to tatters, to very rags, to split the ears of the groundlings, who for the most part are capable of nothing but inexplicable dumb-shows and noise.*
>
> *Hamlet*, Act III, Scene II

The poor old groundlings… Although, some might say that being so close to the actors meant the groundlings had the best seat in the house. (Except they had no seat. And it was a theatre and not a house. But hey ho.)

Fantastic play tonight Jack

Top notch!

Verdict: _____ TRUTH

THE BARD'S BEST BITS
(But what did Shakespeare mean?)

THE PLAY: THE TEMPEST

> **Prospero:** We are such stuff as dreams are made on, rounded with a little sleep. (Act IV: Scene I)

We are made of dreams, and our lives start and end with sleep.

> **Miranda:** O wonder!
> How many goodly creatures are there here!
> How beauteous mankind is! O, brave new world,
>
> That has such people in't!
>
> (Act V: Scene I)

Wow. How many lovely creatures there are here! They are soooo beautiful. What a fabulous new world this is to have such people in it!

(FYI, Miranda doesn't really mean what she says. She's being ironic. These are the first new people she's seen for years and they're actually drunken sailors, not beautiful people at all. Just imagine her saying this with one raised eyebrow and you've got her tone.)

Caliban:

Be not afeard; the isle is full of noises,

Sounds, and sweet airs, that give delight and hurt not.

Sometimes a thousand twangling instruments

Will hum about mine ears; and sometime voices,

That, if I then had waked after long sleep,

Will make me sleep again: and then, in dreaming,

The clouds methought would open, and show riches

Ready to drop upon me; that, when I waked,

I cried to dream again. (Act III: Scene II)

Really short translation: It's fab here. You'll love it. I do.

Bonus fact!

Author Aldous Huxley borrowed Shakespeare's words for the title of his 1931 book **Brave New World**. Like the character Miranda, Huxley was being ironic too, because the world in his classic novel is really not very nice at all.

Shakespeare lived a double life

Introducing... **Shakespeare Number One!**

He was a top playwright and actor, who lived in London. You might have heard of him. He wrote a lot of tragic, historical and very funny plays. He was officially FAMOUS.

Now let's meet... **Shakespeare Number Two!**

He was a well known and highly respected man of property with a wife and three children, who he visited in his home town of Stratford. He was RICH.

Which one is the REAL Shakespeare?

 And the truth is...

Both Shakespeare Number One and Shakespeare Number Two were totally real.

Phew. He was a busy man!

Verdict: _____ TRUTH

86

DIDST THOU KNOW?

If you shuffle the letters of WILLIAM SHAKESPEARE, it spells

'I AM A WEAKISH SPELLER'.
(No wonder he couldn't spell his own name – see page 66.)

It also spells:

HEAR ME AS I WILL SPEAK

and

I'LL MAKE A WISE PHRASE

Why not have a go yourself? There are so many common letters in WILLIAM SHAKESPEARE'S name that it's possible to make over 80,000 anagrams from them.

Shakespeare was BANNED

Just imagine banning the plays *Romeo and Juliet* or *Macbeth* from the stage… It's just unthinkable!

⭐ And the truth is…

Well, fasten your seatbelts because it DID actually happen in the 1600s, when Oliver Cromwell and the Puritans were in charge. They thought that theatres encouraged bad behaviour. And they weren't big on 'fun' either.

All theatres were closed in 1642 when civil war broke out. And two years later, The Globe theatre was demolished.

Luckily, theatres were later rebuilt and reopened. And now Shakespeare's plays have been performed countless times.

Phew.

Verdict: 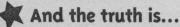 TRUTH

Shakespeare was buried nearly three times as deep as usual

In the UK, when people die their coffins are traditionally buried six feet deep, which is about 1.83 metres. In the USA, it's four feet or 1.23 metres.

So why on earth (pardon the pun) would William Shakespeare be buried an astonishing 17 feet under the ground, which is 5.18 metres (and, Shakespeare and wildlife fans, also the average height of a male giraffe)?

And the truth is...

No one knows for sure if Shakespeare actually IS buried 17 feet deep or not, for the simple reason that no one has ever dug him up.

But why was William Shakespeare buried that deep? The answer lies on page 92...

Verdict: _____ TRUTH (apparently).

Shakespeare put a curse on his own grave!

Shakespeare is buried at the Holy Trinity Church, Stratford-upon-Avon, England, which is the town where he was born and died. But VIPs are often buried in grand cathedrals, so why not Probably The World's Greatest Playwright Ever?

★ And the truth is...

In Shakespeare's day, gravediggers often dug up the dead, either for research or to make room for new bodies. Shakespeare felt strongly about this practice and so, to put off prospective gravediggers and to make sure that he didn't move anywhere once he was dead, Shakespeare asked that an inscription be carved onto his tomb (see right). So perhaps this is why no one's ever moved Shakespeare's bones to a more splendid place... They didn't DARE.

GOOD FREND FOR JESUS SAKE FOREBEARE,

TO DIGG THE DUST ENCLOASED HEARE;

BLESTE BE THE MAN THAT SPARES THES STONES,

AND CURST BE HE THAT MOVES MY BONES.

Bonus fact!

But in 1741, a memorial statue was erected in Shakespeare's honour in Poets' Corner of Westminster Abbey in London.

Verdict: **TRUTH**

shakespeare died a poor man

Well, that's what usually happens, isn't it? Fabulously creative types are NEVER recognised for their achievements during their actual lifetimes.*

Take Oscar Wilde, the author with the genius wit who died penniless in 1900, for example. Or Vincent Van Gogh, the artist whose paintings sell today for millions, but made less than £100 when he was alive. And then there's poor Jane Austen, who was only 41 when she died; she never knew *Pride and Prejudice* and her other brilliant novels would bring worldwide fame.

Did the same happen to William Shakespeare?

 And the truth is...

Not a bit of it. Will Shakespeare achieved both fame and fortune during his lifetime.

Bravo!

Verdict: —— BUSTED ——

Actually, quite a lot of people DO become famous during their lifetimes. But before the internet and television, it did take a little longer for word to spread.

Where can I find myths about...

100%
SUCKER-PROOF

GUARANTEED!

Take a look at our other marvellously mythbusting titles...

Tip:
Turn over!